African Americans in the Civil War

Untold History of the Civil War

African Americans in the Civil War

Civil War Forts

The Civil War in the West

Civil War Medicine

Ironclads and Blockades in the Civil War

Prison Camps in the Civil War

Rangers, Jayhawkers, and Bushwackers
in the Civil War

Secret Weapons in the Civil War

The Soldier's Life in the Civil War

Spies in the Civil War

The Underground Railroad and the Civil War

Women in the Civil War

CHELSEA HOUSE PUBLISHERS

Untold History of the Civil War

African Americans in the Civil War

Victor Brooks

CHELSEA HOUSE PUBLISHERS
Philadelphia

Produced by Combined Publishing
P.O. Box 307, Conshohocken, Pennsylvania 19428
1-800-418-6065
E-mail:combined@combinedpublishing.com
web:www.combinedpublishing.com

CHELSEA HOUSE PUBLISHERS

Editor in Chief: Stephen Reginald
Managing Editor: James D. Gallagher
Production Manager: Pamela Loos
Art Director: Sara Davis
Director of Photography: Judy L. Hasday
Senior Production Editor: LeeAnne Gelletly
Assistant Editor: Anne Hill

Front Cover Illustration: Courtesy of The Lincoln Museum, Fort Wayne, IN (#4088a)

The Chelsea House World Wide Web site address is
http://www.chelseahouse.com

First Printing

135798642

Library of Congress Cataloging-in-Publication Data applied for:
ISBN 0-7910-5435-7

Contents

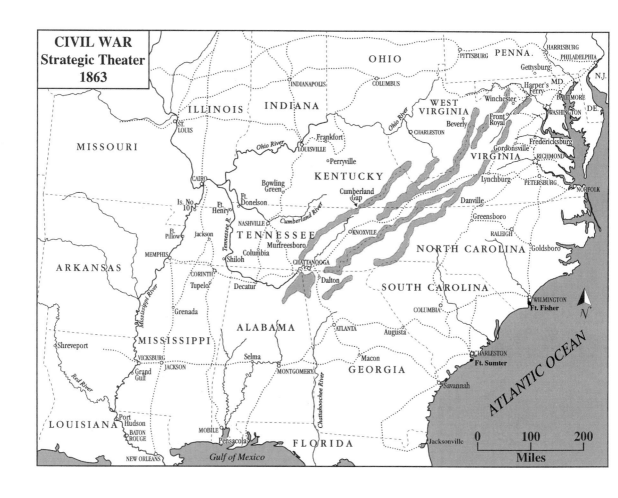

CIVIL WAR
Strategic Theater
1863

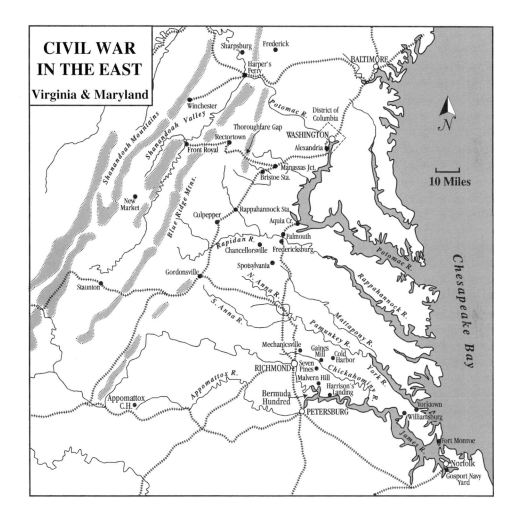

**CIVIL WAR
IN THE EAST**

Virginia & Maryland

Sharpsburg

Frederick

BALTIMORE

Harper's
Ferry

Potomac R.

Winchester

District of
Columbia

Shanandoah Mountains

Shanandoah Valley

Thoroughfare Gap

WASHINGTON

Rectortown

Alexandria

Front Royal

Manassas Jct.

Bristoe Sta.

10 Miles

New
Market

Blue Ridge Mtns.

Culpepper

Rappahannock Sta.

Aquia Cr.

Falmouth

Rapidan R.

Chancellorsville

Fredericksburg

Staunton

Spotsylvania

Potomac R.

Gordonsville

N. Anna R.

Rappahannock R.

Chesapeake Bay

S. Anna R.

Mattapony R.

Mechanicsville

Pamunkey R.

Gaines
Mill

Cold
Harbor

Seven
Pines

RICHMOND

Chickahominy R.

Malvern Hill

York R.

Appomattox R.

Harrison's
Landing

Appomattox
C.H.

Bermuda
Hundred

Yorktown

PETERSBURG

Williamsburg

James R.

Fort Monroe

Norfolk

Gosport Navy
Yard

Civil War Chronology

1860
November 6   Abraham Lincoln is elected president of the United States.

December 20   South Carolina becomes the first state to secede from the Union.

1861
January-April   Mississippi, Florida, Alabama, Georgia, Louisiana, and Texas also secede from the Union.

April 1   Bombardment of Fort Sumter begins the Civil War.

April-May   Lincoln calls for volunteers to fight the Southern rebellion, causing a second wave of secession with Virginia, Arkansas, Tennessee, and North Carolina all leaving the Union.

May   Union naval forces begin blockading the Confederate coast and reoccupying some Southern ports and offshore islands.

July 21   Union forces are defeated at the battle of First Bull Run and withdraw to Washington.

1862
February   Previously unknown Union general Ulysses S. Grant captures Confederate garrisons in Tennessee at Fort Henry (February 6) and Fort Donelson (February 16).

March 7-8   Confederates and their Cherokee allies are defeated at Pea Ridge, Arkansas.

March 8-9   Naval battle at Hampton Roads, Virginia, involving the USS *Monitor* and the CSS *Virginia* (formerly the USS *Merrimac*) begins the era of the armored fighting ship.

April-July   The Union army marches on Richmond after an amphibious landing. Confederate forces block Northern advance in a series of battles. Robert E. Lee is placed in command of the main Confederate army in Virginia.

April 6-7   Grant defeats the Southern army at Shiloh Church, Tennessee, after a costly two-day battle.

April 27   New Orleans is captured by Union naval forces under Admiral David Farragut.

May 31   The battle of Seven Pines (also called Fair Oaks) is fought and the Union lines are held.

August 29-30   Lee wins substantial victory over the Army of the Potomac at the battle of Second Bull Run near Manassas, Virginia.

September 17   Union General George B. McClellan repulses Lee's first invasion of the North at Antietam Creek near Sharpsburg, Maryland, in the bloodiest single day of the war.

November 13   Grant begins operations against the key Confederate fortress at Vicksburg, Mississippi.

December 13   Union forces suffer heavy losses storming Confederate positions at Fredericksburg, Virginia.

1863
January 1   President Lincoln issues the Emancipation Proclamation, freeing the slaves in the Southern states.

May 1-6	Lee wins an impressive victory at Chancellorsville, but key Southern commander Thomas J. "Stonewall" Jackson dies of wounds, an irreplaceable loss for the Army of Northern Virginia.
June	The city of Vicksburg and the town of Port Hudson are held under siege by the Union army. They surrender on July 4.
July 1-3	Lee's second invasion of the North is decisively defeated at Gettysburg, Pennsylvania.
July 16	Union forces led by the black 54th Massachusetts Infantry attempt to regain control of Fort Sumter by attacking the Fort Wagner outpost.
September 19-20	Confederate victory at Chickamauga, Georgia, gives some hope to the South after disasters at Gettysburg and Vicksburg.

1864

February 17	A new Confederate submarine, the *Hunley,* attacks and sinks the USS *Housatonic* in the waters off Charleston.
March 9	General Grant is made supreme Union commander. He decides to campaign in the East with the Army of the Potomac while General William T. Sherman carries out a destructive march across the South from the Mississippi to the Atlantic coast.
May-June	In a series of costly battles (Wilderness, Spotsylvania, and Cold Harbor), Grant gradually encircles Lee's troops in the town of Petersburg, Richmond's railway link to the rest of the South.
June 19	The siege of Petersburg begins, lasting for nearly a year until the end of the war.
August 27	General Sherman captures Atlanta and begins the "March to the Sea," a campaign of destruction across Georgia and South Carolina.
November 8	Abraham Lincoln wins reelection, ending hope of the South getting a negotiated settlement.
November 30	Confederate forces are defeated at Franklin, Tennessee, losing five generals. Nashville is soon captured (December 15-16).

1865

April 2	Major Petersburg fortifications fall to the Union, making further resistance by Richmond impossible.
April 3-8	Lee withdraws his army from Richmond and attempts to reach Confederate forces still holding out in North Carolina. Union armies under Grant and Sheridan gradually encircle him.
April 9	Lee surrenders to Grant at Appomattox, Virginia, effectively ending the war.
April 14	Abraham Lincoln is assassinated by John Wilkes Booth, a Southern sympathizer.

Union Army
Army of the Potomac
Army of the James
Army of the Cumberland

Confederate Army
Army of Northern Virginia
Army of Tennessee

I

A Call to Arms

Benjamin Franklin Butler was probably one of the most unlikely looking generals in the entire Civil War. He was bald, overweight, cross-eyed, and wore a uniform covered with dirt and food stains. Although he served in the Union army, he had been a close friend of Confederate president Jefferson Davis. He had also never served a day in the army before 1861. However, when the Civil War began, Benjamin Butler quickly became one of the best-known figures in the nation. Butler was a Democratic congressman from Massachusetts when Fort Sumter surrendered, and he quickly used his political influence to secure an appointment as a brigadier general in the state militia. When Virginia seceded from the union and it looked as if Confederate troops would attack the national capital, it was General Butler who organized a relief force that paraded into Washington and received the personal thanks of President Abraham Lincoln.

By the spring of 1862, Benjamin Butler was again at the right place at the right time. A powerful Yankee

Some of the officers of the 1st Louisiana Native Guard as they appeared in Harper's Weekly *in February of 1863.*

fleet under Admiral David Farragut had just blasted its way through powerful Confederate forts on the Mississippi River and sailed upstream to demand the surrender of New Orleans, the largest city in the Confederacy. However, it would take Union ground troops to actually take control of the city and it was Benjamin Butler who was appointed commander of this occupation force. When General Butler opened his new headquarters in this huge Rebel city, most of the local Confederate regiments that had been assigned to defend the town had fled beyond the state capital at Baton Rouge. But soon after the Federal army occupied the city, Butler was visited by the officers of three regiments of Confederates who had remained behind when the city was captured. The Yankee general was astonished when he met a group of articulate, wealthy, African-American residents of New Orleans, who, ironically, wore the gray uniforms of Confederate officers.

When the Confederate states had begun raising regiments to defend the South after Lincoln's call for Union volunteers to restore the Federal government, a number of influential blacks had gone to the governor of Louisiana and offered to raise three regiments of free blacks to join the state's militia forces. The governor had quickly accepted this offer, and by the summer of 1861, three regiments of the Louisiana Native Guards were drilling in the parks and squares of New Orleans. These men decided to remain in the city when the Yankees arrived the next spring. While these free blacks were far better-off than the millions of African Americans who were toiling in slavery in the South, they were still very much second-class citizens in a Confederate nation based on white supremacy. The Union cause seemed to offer more hope for some improvement of the African-American condition in the South and many of these black Confederates now offered their services to the Federal government.

Benjamin Butler's first response to this offer to provide three regiments of African American volunteers for the Union army in New Orleans was at first politely refused. However, when Rebel counterattacks threatened to push the undermanned Yankee army out of Louisiana, the politician-turned-general suddenly changed his mind. When Butler pleaded with the War Department in Washington to rush him thousands of reinforcements he was told he was on his own. Since the government would not supply him with more white troops, he insisted, "I will enlist all the colored troops I can from the free Negroes."

The Massachusetts general was not yet prepared to enlist Southern slaves into the Union army guarding

The 1st Louisiana Native Guard disembarking at Fort Macombe, Louisiana.

New Orleans, but on September 27, 1862, the 1st Regiment Louisiana Native Guards became the first African-American regiment to enter United States service in the Civil War. Unlike many regiments recruited later, all of the platoon commanders and company commanders in this regiment were black and when two or more regiments were mustered in, most of their lieutenants and captains were also African Americans. An agent for the Federal government who was visiting New Orleans at the time wrote that "the company officers of these regiments are educated men and each speaks at least two languages. I found that I was conversing with men and of ordinary knowledge and mental capacity."

Once the regiments were fully enlisted in the Federal army, they were sent to Camp Strong Station four miles north of New Orleans, where they were armed and given basic training. One of General Butler's staff officers recognized the huge potential of using these black men to help beat the Confederacy. He insisted, "Better soldiers never shouldered arms. They were zealous, obedient, and intelligent. No men in the Union army had such a stake in the contest as they. Few understood it as well as they."

These 1,200 Louisiana African Americans who drilled and trained on a dusty campground near New Orleans were the first of almost 180,000 black soldiers who would serve in the Union army during the Civil War. These first volunteers and the black men who would follow them would endure the same hardships and dangers as white soldiers of the time. They had to deal with food that was often spoiled and crawling

The 20th United States Colored Troops received their flag in Union Square in New York before going off to war.

with worms, primitive medical care, and battle tactics that caused unbelievably high casualties. Over 60,000 of these men would die from either disease or enemy bullets. Beyond the problems they shared with their white counterparts, these African-American bluecoats faced other special challenges. For much of the war they were paid less than white soldiers even though they faced the same dangers. They were much more likely to be hanged or shot after they surrendered to Southern soldiers since the Confederate government often branded them "insurrectionists," who shouldn't be treated as prisoners of war. They also had to convince many Yankee generals that they were just as able to fight in pitched battles as white regiments. None of these tasks were easy, but as the war dragged on year after year and more and more African Americans shouldered muskets and entered the battlefield, people in the North, and even many in the South began to realize that the war would not be won or lost by white Americans alone. Within a few weeks after those first black Louisianans put on their blue uniforms for the first time, they traded shots with other men from Louisiana who had joined the Rebel cause. Once these first battles were fought, the course of the Civil War would never be the same.

ROBERT SMALLS

FIRST AFRICAN AMERICAN TO COMMAND A SHIP IN THE UNITED STATES NAVY

Born in 1839 in Beaufort, South Carolina, Robert Smalls received a rudimentary education as a young man, learning to read. In 1851, his master moved to Charleston, where Smalls was permitted to work for day wages on the docks as a deck hand. He became a skilled steersman and harbor pilot.

At the outbreak of the Civil War, Smalls, who by then was married and had two children, was pressed into service with the Confederate navy. In April 1862, he was assigned as a steersman and pilot of the armed transport *Planter*, and his brother, John, was made chief engineer. Save for the captain and two other officers, the entire ship's crew was composed of slaves. The *Planter*, which was armed with six cannons, normally carried goods and supplies to the various forts and installations in the vicinity of Charleston Harbor, including the famous Fort Sumter.

Almost as soon as he came aboard, Smalls began to plot an escape.

In the early hours of May 13, 1862, the *Planter* lay at her normal berth, near army headquarters on the Charleston waterfront, with the captain and the other white officers ashore. While John touched off the boilers, Smalls smuggled their wives and four children aboard, as well as the wife of one of the other crewmen. As soon as steam was up, Smalls took the ship out into the harbor.

Steaming at a leisurely pace, the *Planter* attracted no attention. A familiar sight, none of the troops on guard thought anything amiss as it steamed by the various harbor installations, the Confederate flag

proudly streaming behind and its whistle giving the appropriate call signs. As soon as the ship was out of range of the last Confederate batteries at Fort Sumter, Smalls ordered full speed and headed for the blockading Union warships. When one of the blockaders approached, Smalls hauled down the Confederate colors and hoisted a large white bed sheet.

Smalls's exploit brought him considerable fame in the North. It also made him a prosperous man, for as captain he received a sizeable share of the prize money which was awarded to those who captured an enemy vessel. Meanwhile, Lincoln appointed him a pilot in the navy. He served on a number of vessels and was cited for courage under fire while serving on the monitor *Keokuk* during the naval assault on Charleston in April 1863. That December he was made master of a small ship of his own serving on blockade duty, and thus became the first black man to command a ship in the United States Navy.

*President Abraham Lincoln signed the Emancipation
Proclamation, January 1, 1863.*

II

Liberating the Mississippi

*J*anuary 1, 1863, dawned clear and cold in Washington, D.C., and by late morning thousands of the capital's citizens were lining up at the gates of the White House to take part in a traditional event, the president's New Year's open house. Abraham Lincoln stood by a small table in the Blue Room and shook hands with hundreds of common citizens. Then, soon after the reception ended, the president went upstairs to his office and in the presence of most of his cabinet signed one of the most important documents in American history, the Emancipation Proclamation. The presidential order declared that "all persons held as slaves within any state or designated part of a state, the people whereof shall then be in rebellion against the United States shall be then, thenceforward, and forever free."

This revolutionary document would only take full effect if the Union won the Civil War and on New Years' Day of 1863 that result was far from certain. The main Union army in the East, the Army of the

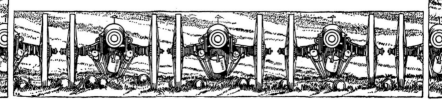

Following the Emancipation Proclamation many blacks fled to the Union lines.

Potomac, had just endured one of its worst defeats of the war at Fredericksburg, Virginia, and the main Yankee army in Tennessee was at the time fighting for its life along the muddy fields of Stones River. However, the most important campaign up to this point in the war was underway far to the west along the Mississippi River, and Abraham Lincoln knew that the result of that struggle could very well determine the outcome of the war. Ever since the Southern states had seceded, the lower Mississippi River had been closed to midwestern states' commerce. Federal armies had captured large stretches of the shoreline of the river during 1862, but a vital 150-mile stretch of the Mississippi between Port Hudson, Louisiana, and Vicksburg, Mississippi, was still under Confederate

The 1st South Carolina Volunteers stand in formation at Port Royal, South Carolina. They were the first unit of former slaves to officially enlist.

control. As long as the Rebels held this territory, the Confederate states west of the Mississippi could pour cattle, cotton, supplies, and soldiers across the river to support the eastern states that desperately needed all of these items. Abraham Lincoln himself admitted "the war can never be brought to a close until that key is in our pocket." Now a huge campaign was underway to capture that key and a number of African-American regiments would play an important part in the dramatic events that were about to happen.

As the winter of 1863 ended and the spring campaigning season began, Union armies started to advance toward the two main Confederate strongholds on the Mississippi River. One army under General Ulysses S. Grant moved downstream from

Memphis to threaten the city of Vicksburg while another army moved upstream from New Orleans to attack Port Hudson. The commander of this second army was General Nathaniel Banks who had succeeded Benjamin Butler during the winter. General Banks was, like Butler, a Massachusetts politician who had been appointed as a general for political reasons. Banks had been governor of Massachusetts and eventually speaker of the house in Congress and he now believed that a spectacular military victory just might carry him into the White House. Unfortunately, while Banks was a very talented politician, he was not a very good general as both the black and white troops under his command would soon discover.

General Banks's main assignment as commander of the Department of the Gulf was to capture the Rebel held river port of Port Hudson while General Grant was marching against Vicksburg. On May 21, 1863, the black 1st and 3rd Regiments of Louisiana Native Guards, along with a number of white units, began marching north from Baton Rouge toward the enemy lines around Port Hudson. A torrid sun beat down on the dusty roads while there was very little drinking water along the route. Five days later the two regiments were in position on the extreme right of the Union siege line with an all-out assault planned the next day. The African-American soldiers were part of a large Yankee attack force that circled the land side of the town but the bluecoats faced two huge disadvantages. First, Confederate engineers had constructed a powerful series of fortifications bristling with cannons, all positioned to pour their lethal fire on the few roads that cut through the swampy ground. The Federals would have to charge straight down these roads under a hail of Rebel fire. Second, General Banks had so little military experience that he had no

General Nathaniel Banks led the assault on Port Hudson in which the black Louisiana Native Guards finally saw battle.

idea how to create diversions or keep the enemy guessing about the direction of his attack. He simply ordered a huge charge and hoped for the best.

At dawn on May 27, 1863, Brigadier General William Dwight organized the two brigades of his division to prepare to attack the Confederate positions along Big Sandy Creek. His attack force included the two African American regiments, a regiment of Louisiana cavalrymen who had sided with the Union, infantry regiments from New York and Massachusetts, and a single pair of cannons from a Massachusetts artillery battery. Dwight was convinced that the Louisiana blacks would make excellent soldiers and asked for them to be put into his division. The African-American troops were determined to prove that he had made the right decision. While General Banks had replaced most of the black officers in the 3rd Regiment with his own white friends, the 1st Regiment still contained a large number of African-American officers, mostly with French names. One company commander, Captain André Cailloux, was considered one of the finest horsemen in Louisiana while other officers were wealthy merchants and professionals.

At 8 A.M. on a typically torrid Southern summer morning, the Union attack lurched into motion after the Federal navy had bombarded the Rebel positions from the Mississippi River. General Dwight's task force marched rapidly down the Telegraph Road and clambered over a newly constructed pontoon bridge that crossed the Big Sandy Creek. However, as soon as the bluecoats crossed to the other side, dozens of gray-coats opened fire from concealed rifle pits and killed or wounded large numbers of Federal troops. When the two Yankee cannons were advanced to support the Union infantry, six hidden Confederate guns opened fire and smashed the Federal battery to pieces.

As black and white Federal troops dropped all around them, Captain Cailloux and other officers moved among the ranks of their men, steadying them with words of encouragement in both French and English. Much of the most destructive Rebel fire was coming from a small ridge running parallel to the road and the Louisiana African Americans were assigned to take that high ground. A white officer watching the daring attack marveled at the troops' ability to hold together while taking high casualties and he insisted, "valiantly did the heroic descendants of Africa move forward, cool as if marshaled for dress parade."

Captain Cailloux had his arm mangled by a Rebel artillery shell part way through the charge but he switched his sword to his other hand and continued toward the Confederate cannons. A moment later the captain went down with a fatal wound and several other officers soon were on the ground around him.

As each attack on the Rebel lines wavered, General Dwight organized a new assault with a smaller and smaller force of bluecoats. A reporter for a New Orleans newspaper noted that "especially in the two black regiments, there were several instances of wounded men returning to the field after their wounds had been dressed and fighting for the balance of the day." Dwight insisted that the attacks continue "until there is only a corporal's guard left. When there is only one man left, let him come to me and report." However, General Banks was shocked at the losses to

This illustration was printed in Harper's Weekly *of the funeral of Captain André Cailloux, a black company commander from Louisiana. In the article accompanying the sketch they called him "one of the bravest soldiers in our country's service."*

his army; almost 2,000 Union men were killed or wounded at a loss of only about 200 graycoats. Of all the units in Banks army, only one white regiment had more men killed in action than the 1st Louisiana. By the time that Banks called off the assault, over 300 African-American troops were dead or badly wounded. A Yankee soldier who would later serve as an officer in a black regiment insisted, "the negroes fought like devils, they made fine charges on a battery that there was not the slightest chance of their taking. They have showed our boys that they could and would fight." A New York soldier who had been part of the bloody attack noted that "they charged and re-charged and didn't know what retreat meant. They make splendid soldiers and are as good fighting men as any we have."

The bloody assault on Port Hudson convinced General Banks that it would be better to simply besiege the Rebel garrison and capture the city when the Rebels were out of food. A costly attack on Vicksburg at about the same time had convinced General Grant to do the same thing around that town and so the whole success of the Union plan depended on preventing either Confederate garrison from getting supplies from the far side of the Mississippi River. A number of Federal units, including several African-American regiments, were assigned the task of keeping enemy reinforcements and supplies from the two Confederate strongholds while the Southern generals became equally determined to save their comrades at Port Hudson and Vicksburg.

One of the key points along the Yankee line of forts on the Mississippi River was at Milliken's Bend, Louisiana. This small docking area on a bend of the river was established as both a link in the Federal siege lines and a training base for new units of African

Americans that were now being recruited into the Union army. By early June, four regiments of African Americans, three units from Louisiana and one from Mississippi, were being organized near the supply depot while a small number of white soldiers from Iowa and Illinois provided security for the huge stockpiles of supplies that were stored there. As Confederate leaders desperately looked for some way to break the sieges of Port Hudson and Vicksburg, Confederate General Edmund Kirby Smith came up with the idea of a series of Rebel attacks that would destroy most of the Union supply depots and force the Yankee armies to either retreat or starve. Confederate scouts had reported to General Smith that Milliken's Bend was one of the most vulnerable links in the Yankee line as "it is guarded by convalescents and negroe troops and no danger is anticipated." Therefore on June 7, 1863, a Rebel assault force formed into ranks and launched a noisy, howling charge on the outnumbered Federals.

Colonel Herman Lieb, the commanding officer at Milliken's Bend depot realized he was in serious trouble when Union pickets rushed in with news that a

This illustration depicts the battle at Milliken's Bend, June 7, 1863. General Grant said of the black troops who fought there, "Their conduct is said to have been most gallant."

Newly recruited black soldiers were quickly given instructions on the use of their weapons and then thrown into battle.

huge Rebel force was heading for the Yankee camp. While the three brigades of Texas infantry moving on Milliken's Bend were almost all veteran troops, the African-American Unionists had been soldiers for only two weeks. Many of the black troops had just received their weapons and had never fired a musket. Lieb's only hope was to pull his untrained men back to a six-foot-high levee about 150 yards from the river bank and hope that reinforcements arrived before his men were slaughtered.

The Confederate attack on the Yankees was simply a brutal frontal assault with long rows of graycoats wielding bayonets that glistened in the sun. Since many of the Federals had only received their muskets the day before, they loaded their awkward weapons very slowly and the Rebels were able to clamber over the levee wall and pour down on the defenders. When the Rebels swarmed over the walls, the African-American troops placed bayonets on their muskets and began a bloody struggle of hand-to-hand combat. A Union officer insisted that the "yelling, cutting, and slashing for ten or fifteen minutes was terrible. A large black sergeant laid into a group of Texans and smashed in every head he could reach." The Confederates were at first shocked by the fury of what they thought was going to be an easy battle, but the Texans soon had help from gray-coated horse soldiers who managed to get around the end of the levee wall and charge into the Federal troops. A Texan colonel admitted that the black troops had "fought desperate" and revealed that "bayonets were crossed and muskets clubbed and the struggle became a close and deadly one." However, this Rebel officer noted that the Confederates had more men and "after some hard fighting, the black soldiers were driven to the water's edge."

The Union garrison at Milliken's Bend was now in a desperate situation as the bluecoats were now backpedaling to the steep banks of the river with charging Confederates in front and the Mississippi River behind them. But as both black and white Yankees lined up for a last stand help began to arrive. Two Federal navy gunboats steamed into position and began lobbing huge shells into the middle of the charging Rebels. Meanwhile, large numbers of hungry graycoats had abandoned the firing line to plunder the huge Union supply depot. The commander of the Confederate assault force, General Henry McCulloch, now had to make a major decision. He had lost over 200 men in what he had thought would be an easy pushover attack. Lines of mostly African-American bluecoats were now backed up by powerful naval vessels that could possibly smash any final assault. Finally, the Texan general decided that the risk wasn't worth it and ordered his men to retreat westward.

The 1,100 Federal troops who had defended Milliken's Bend had suffered over 400 casualties defending the Union depot and almost 350 of these men were African American. The bravery of these troops soon came to the attention of General Ulysses S. Grant. The commanding general of this campaign reported, "In this battle most of the troops engaged were Africans who had but little experience in the use of fire arms. Their conduct is said, however, to have been most gallant, and I doubt not but with good officers they will make good troops." Four weeks after General Grant made this report, both Vicksburg and Port Hudson surrendered along with almost 40,000 Confederate troops. African Americans had fought in their first major battles and had proved that they could fight and die as well as the white troops in both armies. Along with their white comrades they could rejoice in participating in one of the most decisive campaigns of the Civil War as Abraham Lincoln noted, referring to the great Mississippi River, "The Father of Waters now goes unvexed to the sea." As citizens throughout the North celebrated the Union victory in the Vicksburg campaign, a regiment of African Americans from the northern states was about to carve out an even more dramatic piece of Civil War glory.

H. M. Turner

First African American commissioned as a chaplain in the United States Military

H. M. Turner was born in 1832 in South Carolina. As a young boy, he took on the difficult task of teaching himself to read as the laws of the state prohibited blacks from receiving an education. Eventually Turner's obvious intelligence caught the attention of some lawyers he was working for and they in turn defied the laws of the state and gave him an education.

When Turner was 17 years old he joined the Methodist Church becoming a preacher at the young age of 20. Turner's first sermon was so inspiring and intelligent that he began to attract crowds wherever he preached throughout the South. He eventually ended up assigned to the Israel Bethel Church in Washington, D.C. There his reputation rose and it was not unusual to see several congressmen sitting in his congregation.

Turner took up the cause of enlisting blacks as soldiers for the Union army. He and others who backed this controversial cause persisted until the 1st United States Colored Regiment was formed. On September 10, 1863, Turner was commissioned as chaplain of the new regiment. In *Harper's Weekly* Turner was praised as "a man of great personal courage." The 1st U.S. Colored Regiment went on to distinguish themselves as brave soldiers of the Union.

This painting depicts the storming of Fort Wagner by the 54th Massachusetts Infantry, July 18, 1863.

III

Glory at Fort Wagner

*A*t dawn, on May 28, 1863, only hours after the 1st Louisiana Native Guards had become the first large force of African Americans to see combat in the Civil War, almost a thousand blue-coated soldiers marched out of Camp Meigs, Massachusetts, and boarded railroad cars for the short trip into downtown Boston. This Thursday was turning into a beautiful New England spring day and when the young soldiers arrived in the city there was a huge crowd gathered to watch the men march through town to their final destination of Battery Wharf. While so many other Massachusetts regiments had received enthusiastic send-offs as they embarked on their quest to restore the Union, this day was particularly special. The enlisted troops of this new regiment, the 54th Massachusetts Infantry, were all African Americans who had been recruited from throughout the North to fight the Confederacy, and everyone who watched this regiment march by knew that this was no ordinary unit.

Frederick Douglass, the famous abolitionist, encouraged the War Department to raise a regiment of free blacks which became the 54th Massachusetts Infantry.

The 54th Massachusetts was largely the idea of Massachusetts' Republican governor John Andrew who had been one of the most vocal early supporters of recruiting African Americans to help defeat the Rebels. Governor Andrew, with strong support from Frederick Douglass, Harriet Beecher Stowe, and other famous abolitionists, had convinced the War Department to go along with his plan to raise a regiment of free blacks from Massachusetts, but only on condition that all officers' slots would be reserved for whites. The governor immediately began searching

A recruiting poster encouraging blacks to join the Union army.

for men from influential families to accept commissions in the regiment to give the new unit credibility. He found an excellent colonel for the unit when 25-year-old Robert Gould Shaw, a member of one of Boston's leading families, agreed to accept command. Junior officers included men like Lieutenant Garth James, younger brother of writers Henry James and William James, and the enlisted ranks included two of Frederick Douglass's sons, Lewis and Charles. Since Massachusetts did not have a large enough African-American population to easily fill out the whole regiment, recruiting agents went to New York, Philadelphia, Chicago, and even Canada to recruit men for the new project. After spending most of the spring of 1863 in basic training, by late May the 54th Massachusetts was ready to go into action.

Colonel Robert Gould Shaw led the attack of the black 54th Massachusetts Infantry against Fort Wagner.

When the enthusiastic soldiers marched through Boston and boarded the steamer *De Molay* they found out that their destination was South Carolina. This news sent a chill of excitement through many of the men as that state had one of the largest slave populations in the South and had been the place where the secession movement had first started. The men of the 54th Massachusetts were now involved in an operation to capture Charleston and raise the flag once again over Fort Sumter, the scene of the first battle of the war two years earlier. Henry Gooding, an African American from New Bedford, Massachusetts, who had given up a secure maritime job to join the Union army admitted that this would be a very dangerous adventure. He insisted, "there is not a man in the regiment who does not appreciate the difficulties, the dangers and maybe ignoble death that awaits him. But when a thousand men are fighting for a very existence . . . the greatest difficulty will be to stop them."

By the time the 54th Massachusetts arrived in South Carolina, General Quincy Gillmore had assembled a force of over 15,000 Yankee soldiers supported by a large fleet of naval ironclads. Once the Union army had established a base on Folly Island, eight miles south of Charleston, General Gillmore and his naval counterpart, Admiral John Dahlgren, put together their attack plan. The key to Confederate defense of Charleston Harbor was Fort Sumter and a few weeks earlier a naval assault on that legendary fort had failed miserably. Gillmore and Dahlgren agreed that Sumter could only be safely attacked by army siege guns firing from the tip of nearby Morris Island about a mile away from the Confederate stronghold. However, very near the north end of Morris Island Rebel engineers had built a powerful sand and dirt strongpoint called Fort Wagner. Until the Stars and Stripes were flying over Fort Wagner, Fort Sumter and the city of Charleston would remain in Confederate hands.

The main Union offensive against Fort Wagner began on the morning of July 16, 1863, when several Federal regiments were ferried to James Island which was the next piece of land over from Morris Island and the enemy fort. When the men of the 54th Massachusetts were landed at this jump-off position they were quickly pressed into action. The Confederate commander of Charleston, General Pierre Beauregard, was determined to break up the Yankee assault on Morris Island before it got fully underway, and on this sultry Thursday afternoon a combined force of Rebel horse soldiers and riflemen came storming out of the swamps to smash the Yankee rear guard. The graycoats smashed into Colonel Shaw and three companies of the 54th Massachusetts. The Boston colonel had trained his men well, and the African-American Yankees quickly formed firing lines and opened up a sheet of fire on the screaming Confederates. In a brutal hand-to-hand struggle with clubbed muskets, bayonets, and even fists swinging wildly, 45 of the Massachusetts men went down killed or wounded, but the Rebel officers called off the attack and pulled back into the swampy forest from which they had come.

The next morning, the African-American troops were ferried over to the southern tip of Morris Island in a perfectly executed amphibious landing. Soon 41 siege mortars and heavy cannons had been put in position about 1,000 yards from Fort Wagner and a storm of shells began to pour down on the Rebel stronghold.

General Gillmore hoped to smash the Confederate fortress with the use of artillery alone, but he gradually realized that the fort might have to be taken by storm. Brigadier General George Strong, a fiery 31-year-old Vermonter, was put in charge of the Union assault and the young general promptly asked his fellow New Englander, Colonel Shaw, if the 54th Massachusetts was willing to lead the attack. The commander of the 54th had very mixed feelings about accepting this assignment for his men. On the one hand, this assault could very well provide enormous publicity for this new regiment and prove that the 54th Massachusetts might become one of the best fighting forces in the Union army. On the other hand, the regiment that led this desperate assault would probably suffer very heavy casualties and many of Shaw's men might not survive the attack. But Colonel Shaw accepted the challenge and ordered his men to prepare for action.

On Saturday, July 18, the men of the 54th Massachusetts sat among the sand dunes and waited to launch their night assault. Sergeant Henry Gooding, who had grown up in Massachusetts, complained about the sultry weather as "the heat was enough to make a fellow contemplate the place for the ungodly." Another sergeant wrote his mother that he asked God "to protect me through this, my first fiery trial." Finally, around 6 P.M., the cannonade stopped and the African-American soldiers marched up to the Union siege line. As waves lapped up against the beach where the men were standing, Yankee officers debated their chances of taking Fort Wagner. While General Gillmore was convinced that his artillery had

significantly reduced the 1,300 men and 30 cannons defending the Confederate fort, one of the brigade commanders, Colonel Haldimand Putnam, insisted the attack was suicide as "we are all going into Wagner like a flock of sheep."

Hundreds of brave men from the 54th Massachusetts Infantry gave their lives in the assault of Fort Wagner.

Just as the sun began to set on this long, summer day, the men of the 54th Massachusetts were ordered into formation and instructed to advance along the stretch of sandy beach between the Yankee siege guns and the walls of Fort Wagner. At first, no cannons from the Confederate fort greeted the bluecoat attackers, but artillery from Rebel positions on Sullivan Island, James Island, and Fort Sumter spouted flame and soon shells were dropping into the Federal ranks. Sergeant Lewis Douglass noted proudly, "not a man flinched although it was a trying time. Men fell all around me. A shell would explode and clear a space of twenty feet, our men would close up again." The surviving African-American soldiers broke into a run as they closed within 100 yards of Fort Wagner, and almost at that moment three regiments of graycoats in the fort let loose with every musket and cannon that could fire. Sergeant Douglass called the fire "a perfect hail of shot and shell" while one of the officers insisted "the enemy fire mowed our men down by the hundreds."

As the Massachusetts troops reached a shallow moat in front of Fort Wagner, Sergeant William Carney found the soldier entrusted with the regiment's national colors sprawled dead in the sand. Carney grabbed the flag, splashed across the moat, and started to scramble up the fort's front wall as "grape canisters and hand grenades came down in storms." Sergeant George Stephens, a cabinetmaker from Philadelphia, made it to the top of the wall along with Sergeant Carney but noticed that most of the men in his platoon "were all falling and rolling down the slope into the ditch, while I had my sword sheath blown away when I reached the parapet." At about the same time, Colonel Shaw reached the top of Fort Wagner's walls and furiously waved his sword to encourage his men to keep climbing up. A moment later he was fatally wounded and tumbling down the sandy slope. Sergeant Carney, with bullets whizzing past him, kept encouraging his men to advance by waving the flag but few men reached the top uninjured. As the survivors of the 54th Massachusetts engaged in a deadly duel with the Rebel defenders using swords, bayonets, pistols, and rifle butts, men from the follow-up white regiments tried to push through the hail of fire to join the battle.

As supporting regiments of Yankees charged along the narrow beach, with the ocean on one side and swamps on the other flank, they were perfect targets for the gray-coated defenders. Colonel Putnam tried the desperate tactic of ordering his men to wade into the ocean to try to storm the fort from the side, but Rebel snipers killed the Federal colonel and dozens of his men as they splashed through the waves. A few minutes later, General Strong, the commander of the assault force, went down with a mortal wound and the surviving soldiers began to realize that Fort Wagner was not going to be captured on this humid summer night.

Within an hour after the 54th Massachusetts had scrambled up the walls of Fort Wagner, every senior officer in the regiment was dead or wounded and almost half of the men were out of action. Sergeant Carney, who would be the first African American to win the Congressional Medal of Honor, had been badly wounded in the hip, but grimly held the Stars and Stripes as he backpedaled out of the fort, remarking proudly, "the old flag never touched the ground." Two hundred and fifty-six men of the 54th Massachusetts regiment were dead or wounded by morning with Colonel Shaw and dozens of his men dumped into a mass grave by Confederate defenders. While the Confederate flag would wave over Fort Wagner for a few more weeks, the survivors of the attack were far from discouraged. Frederick Douglass insisted, "in that terrible battle under the wings of night, more cavils in respect to the equality of Negro manhood were set to rest than could have been during a century of ordinary life." A Union officer who had originally believed that it was a mistake to enlist black soldiers admitted that this battle had changed his mind. "I have changed my opinion of the negroes as soldiers since they showed themselves so efficient in the storming of Fort Wagner." Perhaps the New York *Tribune* best summarized the importance of Fort Wagner to Northern opinion of the role of African Americans in the winning of the Civil War: "Fort Wagner has become such a name to the colored race as Bunker Hill has been for ninety years to white Yankees."

IV

Black Men in Gray

When reports of the fighting abilities of black troops at Port Hudson, Milliken's Bend, and Fort Wagner began to spread across America, not only Northerners began to talk about the advantages of African Americans in uniform. Throughout the South, a growing number of Confederate politicians and officers began debating the possibility of using blacks to fight under the Southern flag. The minority of African Americans who were free residents of the Southern states were involved with Confederate state units very early in the war. Not only had the three regiments of Louisiana Native Guards originally been authorized by the Confederate governor of that state, but in June of 1861 the state of Tennessee had encouraged the enlistment of "all eligible free Negroes" at the same pay rates as white volunteers. The state of Virginia, with the largest number of free blacks in the South was using African-American soldiers as early as the battle of Bull Run, and in that first major battle of the war an artillery unit of black gunners known as the

Illustrations such as this one of Rebel black pickets that appeared in Harper's Weekly *in early 1863 indicated that the Confederate army was enlisting blacks.*

Richmond Howitzers had served with distinction, suffering a number of casualties in the Confederate victory. By late 1862, as the war in Virginia shifted toward the town of Fredericksburg, Northern magazines such as *Harper's Weekly* were carrying illustrations of gray-coated African Americans manning Rebel picket lines. A few months later, before the battle of Chancellorsville, Union General Joseph Hooker was so concerned at seeing groups of more than 50 Confederate blacks at one time that he notified the War Department in Washington that the Rebels might soon be capable of utilizing a huge new source of soldiers.

Throughout the first three years of the Civil War, African Americans living in the Confederacy were used to build fortifications, drive wagons, serve as servants for officers, and in a few cases, serve as riflemen or gunners. While the few free blacks were often treated politely by their white counterparts in uniform, most of the huge number of slaves were kept well away from weapons and used mainly for backbreaking labor that regular Southern troops refused to perform. However by early 1864, as the ranks of graycoats were thinned by casualties and Yankee units were increased by recruiting African Americans, at least some

Confederate leaders began to think seriously about recruiting slaves to become full-fledged Rebel soldiers.

Many blacks served as cooks, wagon drivers, and laborers at the beginning of the war. Only later would they be allowed to serve as soldiers.

The first serious discussion of turning slaves into Confederate soldiers occurred in northern Georgia on a frigid January night in 1864. The Confederate Army of Tennessee was preparing to defend the key city of Atlanta against General William T. Sherman's Yankee army that could field well over twice as many men as the graycoats. However, one of the Rebel army's most talented generals had a plan to even the odds. General Patrick Cleburne was not a native-born Southerner but had emigrated from Ireland to Arkansas before the Civil War. He had become a prosperous lawyer and had moved up rapidly in the ranks of the Rebel army during the past three years. Now the former member of the British army called together his regimental and brigade commanders to discuss how they could fill the depleted ranks of the Confederate army before the Yankees crushed the South. Cleburne's division already was employing large numbers of African-American slaves as cooks, wagon drivers, and laborers, but he was convinced that if these men were offered the reward of freedom for their services, they would become fine combat soldiers. The Irishman noted the excellent fighting skills of the slaves on the island of Santo Domingo who had revolted against French rule there, and insisted that Yankee African Americans were proving to be formidable enemies of the Confederacy in battle. He emphasized to his officers that it was foolish for a South on the point of military disaster to ignore the services of thousands of its people because of the color of their skin. On this cold winter night, Cleburne and almost all of his commanders signed a petition to Confederate president Jefferson Davis to consider the immediate enlistment of slaves as Confederate soldiers with the reward of freedom if they served under the Southern flag.

General Cleburne's petition caused turmoil in both the Army of Tennessee and the Confederate government in Richmond. The army generals were very split over support or rejection of the proposal and the Confederate president forbade continued discussion of the subject in the Rebel army camps for the immediate future. However, President Davis did approach the Confederate Congress with a compromise bill. He proposed enlisting 40,000 black laborers to serve as a construction corps working on Confederate fortifications throughout the South. While free African Americans would be paid $11 a month for their services, slaves would be freed at the war's end as a reward for their loyalty to the Rebel cause. President Davis also said that if the military situation became so desperate that it was a choice between freeing slaves in order to fight the Yankees or defeat, "there seems to be no reason to doubt what should then be our deci-

sion." On March 11, 1864, a version of this bill, called "an act to increase the efficiency of the army," passed the Confederate Congress and for the first time, the government of the Confederacy was committed to the eventual emancipation of at least some slaves in return for their service to the Southern cause.

Black laborers build a stockade fence as part of the Confederate army.

The public reaction to even this indirect use of African-American slaves as Confederate soldiers was very mixed. Governor William Smith of Virginia exclaimed his support for the idea as he insisted, "I do not hesitate to say that I would arm such portion of our able-bodied slave population as may be necessary and put them in the field for the spring campaign." The governor argued that "the Yankees boast they have 200,000 of our slaves in arms against us," and now it was time "to put the negro in the army rather than become slaves ourselves." On the other hand, Senator Howell Cobb of Georgia predicted national and racial suicide if slave soldiers were employed as "you can't trust negroes by themselves, especially don't arm them."

As the bloody year of 1864 ended with one Confederate defeat after another, the opinions of men like Howell Cobb began to be drowned out by the desperation of the Rebel cause. A few days before Christmas, the Confederate secretary of war Judah Benjamin admitted, "we are now fast approaching the time when we should be compelled to use every resource at our command for the defense of our liberties. The Negroes will certainly be made to fight against us if not armed for our defense. If they are to fight for our freedom, they are entitled to their own freedom." Secretary Benjamin's ideas had some impact on Southern willingness to use slaves as soldiers, but the most revered general of the Confederacy had even more influence.

The most famous person in the Confederacy during much of the Civil War was General Robert E. Lee and in February of 1865 a desperate Confederate Congress appointed him commander of all armies in the South. Lee quickly used his new position to urge the recruitment of large numbers of African Americans for service in the shrinking Confederate army. He insisted that "we must decide whether slavery shall be extinguished by our enemies and the slaves used against us or whether we should use them ourselves . . . we should employ them without delay." Many Southerners sided with their general at this desperate moment. The Richmond *Sentinel* argued that "any Negroe who volunteers should be welcomed as a brother in arms to white soldiers," and predicted that after the war these brave African Americans would

"have badges of merit and hold certificates of honor" as Confederate citizens. One of Lee's senior officers, General John Gordon, insisted to civilian lawmakers that "our troops are all in favor of enlisting Negroes, this would greatly encourage the army; if authority were granted to raise 200,000 of them it would do much to stop desertion."

Robert E. Lee's opinion was the deciding factor in this debate, and on March 13, 1865, the Confederate Congress voted to enlist up to 300,000 African Americans between the ages of 18 and 45 in the Confederate army with the same pay, clothes, and rations as white soldiers. During the next few weeks officers were appointed to raise new companies and regiments of black soldiers. Parks and town squares around Richmond were soon filled with companies of black recruits, drilling and learning how to use their rifles. Within a short time some units were already helping to man the trenches around the Confederate

A Rebel captain orders blacks at gunpoint to load a cannon during a battle with Berdan's sharpshooters.

capital. When one part of the Rebel line was stretched dangerously thin, Colonel Scott Shipp was ordered to fill the gap with a battalion made up of three companies of white soldiers recovering from wounds and two companies of black soldiers. The commander of the African-American troops reported to headquarters, "I have great pleasure in stating that my men acted with the utmost promptness and good will. Allow me to state that they behaved in extraordinary acceptable manner."

On April 2, 1865, General Lee wrote a letter to President Davis noting that a large number of Confederate officers and soldiers were applying to receive commissions to lead black units. The Virginia general was optimistic that "more men from such a source might work wonders" for the Southern cause. However, only hours after this message was sent, a huge Yankee force, including thousands of black soldiers, smashed through the overstretched Rebel lines and advanced into Richmond itself. The Confederate government and many of its people had decided at the last minute that their slaves could make excellent soldiers, but now it was too late, and the Stars and Stripes were about to flutter over the Rebel capital for the first time in four long years.

V

Forward to Richmond

A few weeks after General Patrick Cleburne suggested using black troops to save a dying Confederacy, the new commander of the Union armies was ordering the enlistment of tens of thousands of African Americans to insure that the Southern states were back under the Stars and Stripes after one more campaign. General Ulysses Grant was appointed the senior general in the Yankee army in March of 1864, and he quickly began developing plans to destroy the two major remaining Rebel armies that were protecting the vital rail center of Atlanta and the Confederate capital of Richmond. Grant planned to start a huge offensive against both Southern armies on exactly the same day, and to keep hammering both Rebel forces until they were destroyed or surrendered. However, this plan would only work if the attacking armies enjoyed a large superiority in numbers of men over the Confederates.

When the Confederates had forced the surrender of Fort Sumter in the spring of 1861, hundreds of thou-

sands of Northerners had volunteered to fight in the Union army. Most of these men had enlisted for three years, assuming the war would long since be finished by 1864. Now three years had passed and these volunteers were free to go home, but if they did leave, the Union army would fall apart. A combination of reenlistment bonuses, generous leaves to go home and visit, and special new insignia convinced just over half of the men to stay with the army, but thousands of new recruits would be needed to fill the gaps. The excellent record of the African-American regiments in earlier battles now convinced Grant and many other leaders that recruiting dozens of new black regiments could now really help the Union cause.

When General Grant ordered the start of the Virginia campaign to destroy Robert E. Lee's army and capture Richmond, the presence of blacks in the Yankee armies was becoming very noticeable. At the start of the campaign in May of 1864, fourteen infantry regiments, one cavalry regiment, and one artillery regiment were composed of black soldiers with a large number of other units being prepared to enter the army in the near future. General Ambrose Burnside's IX Corps and General Benjamin Butler's Army of the James each had entire black divisions. While these units would serve important roles in the first few weeks of the 1864 campaign, several African-American regiments would almost win the war a few weeks later.

During much of May and June of 1864, General Grant's bluecoats and General Lee's graycoats fought each other in the Virginia countryside in places called the Wilderness, Spotsylvania, and Cold Harbor. While the Union army inched its way toward Richmond, over 60,000 Federal troops were killed or wounded and Lee's army was still between the Yankees and the

The 1st South Carolina Volunteers charged into battle in Georgia.

Confederate capital. Finally, in a desperate gamble, Grant decided to leave a small force north of Richmond to convince Lee that he was still going to attack from that direction. Meanwhile, most of the army would be ferried across the James River and move up from the south against the town of Petersburg. This city was the main rail junction for almost every railroad going into Richmond, and if the

Forty black soldiers of the Army of the James rest after a march near Aikins Landing, Virginia, 1864.

Yankees captured the city, the Confederate capital and Lee's army would be cut off from almost all supplies and the war would practically be over.

One of the key units in the daring plan to attack and capture Petersburg was Brigadier General Edward Hincks's division of the Army of the James. This force was made up entirely of African-American regiments, and in the early hours of June 15, 1864, these men almost ended the Civil War. At dawn on this Wednesday morning, advance units of the black 5th Massachusetts Cavalry rode out of a huge grove of trees and approached one of the most powerful fortifications built during the Civil War. The Confederate government knew that if Petersburg was captured, Richmond was doomed, and a brilliant engineering officer named Charles Dimmock, using thousands of slave laborers, had constructed a 10-mile belt of trenches and forts around the town called the

"Cockade City." Now the works constructed by these black bondsmen were about to be assaulted by other African Americans.

The black troopers dismounted and prepared to attack, soon joined by two regiments of African-American foot soldiers under Colonels John Holman and Samuel Duncan. The dismounted horse soldiers and their infantry counterparts pushed through the dense woods and clambered over dozens of fallen trees. As they cut into a field in front of the Confederate fortification, other units of African-American troops were rushed up to reinforce the assault force and soon, almost 5,000 troops were running rapidly through the fields of Baylor's Farm with thousands of bayonets glistening in the summer sunshine. Sergeant Major Christian Fleetwood of the 4th Regiment United States Colored Troops, remembered "our boys charged at double quick and were met with a heavy fire from the rebels." Graycoated defenders quickly picked off over 100 of the men of the 4th Regiment but the surviving troops were soon over the first line of walls and overrunning a battery of Rebel cannons. A reporter who accompanied the troops noted that "the black soldiers were very much elated with their success" and sprinted quickly toward the next line of Confederate fortifications. Every available Rebel cannon opened fire on the bluecoats, but the Federal troops kept streaming into the trenches and over the walls and battery after battery of Rebel cannons was captured. When one southern battery began to slow up the Yankee attack, a group of men from the 1st Regiment United States Colored Troops fixed bayonets and launched a wild charge. "The boys made a bold charge and as they scaled the fort, the enemy became panic-stricken and ran like deer." A sergeant in the 4th Regiment insisted that his men quickly hit another part of the graycoat line and "swept like a tornado over the works."

The Petersburg fort system was a powerful fortification, but Grant's daring plan was now clearly working. General Lee was still convinced that the Yankee army was north of him, and a relatively small number of graycoats had been assigned to guard Petersburg. While the African-American troops still had to push their way through very strong defenses, they were gaining momentum with each new success. By nightfall on June 15 the black troops and the Army of the James had gained one of the most impressive victories of the war. They had captured nine batteries of Confederate artillery, hundreds of enemy soldiers, and had overrun a huge portion of the Rebel fort system. General Hincks begged his superior, General William "Baldy" Smith, to allow his men to continue their attack right into the city of Petersburg all the way to the town's main rail yards. If these men could capture the rail terminus and then receive support from other units of the Federal army the life expectancy of Richmond under a Confederate flag could be measured in days.

General Hincks knew that his men were on the verge of turning the whole course of the war, and these African-American soldiers were eager for an advance into Petersburg that would capture the vital city. However, "Baldy" Smith's nerve failed him at this crucial moment. He couldn't convince himself that this fabulous opportunity to end the war was real. Instead of ordering an attack that would have captured Petersburg, he ordered the victorious black regiments to pull back to the outer line of trenches and postpone an attack until the next day when thousands of reinforcements would join them. As the disbelieving soldiers were ordered out of the forts they had just

captured, a desperate Robert E. Lee began ordering every available Confederate regiment to board trains in Richmond and ride down to the still uncaptured rail terminus in Petersburg. By the next morning, thousands of fresh Rebel soldiers were manning the Petersburg trenches and every Yankee assault on June 16 was beaten back with heavy losses. While Grant quickly fired "Baldy" Smith for his incompetence, bluecoat soldiers, both black and white, were forced to spend almost 10 more months besieging Petersburg and Richmond.

As General Grant gradually tightened the siege of Richmond during the winter of 1865, many new regiments of African Americans joined the Union army. The black soldiers experienced the danger and privations of the campaign and like their white comrades looked forward to the day when the Stars and Stripes would once again fly over the Confederate capital. Finally, at the beginning of April, the long wait was over. On April 1, the new commander of the Army of

The 1st United States Colored Infantry at Petersburg in the fall of 1864. Many black regiments fought bravely to take this city for the Union.

The 55th Massachusetts Colored Regiment marches in the streets of Richmond.

the James, General Godfrey Weitzel, received reports from his siege lines outside of Richmond that many of the Confederate units facing him were being marched over toward Petersburg to challenge a Yankee advance from that direction. The next afternoon, 14 regiments of African-American troops were ordered to prepare to launch a dawn attack on the main Richmond fortifications.

Before dawn on that fateful Monday morning of April 3, as the soldiers prepared for their attack, thunderous explosions were heard from the direction of

Richmond. One African-American soldier insisted that "column after column of fire ascended from the city." Just as the sun was rising, Colonel Charles Francis Adams Jr., the grandson and great-grandson of American presidents, was ordered to take his regiment of black horse soldiers, the 5th Massachusetts Cavalry, and try to discover what was happening in the enemy lines. Adams and his men soon saw signs of retreating Confederates all along the Rebel lines and the troopers quickly reported their exciting information.

As the sun rose higher on this beautiful spring morning, the two corps of the Army of the James, the white Twenty-Fifth Corps and the black Twenty-Fourth Corps, began a friendly competition to see which unit could reach the city limits first. A newspaper reporter accompanying the advancing Yankees gave the prize to the 36th Regiment of United States Colored Infantry who "with its colors was within the city limits before any other regiment, whether of colored or white troops." Soon thousands of blue-coated soldiers were marching into the enemy capital, a city that had withstood Yankee attacks for four long years. Huge numbers of black residents of the city, and even some pro-Union whites, lined the streets to greet the men carrying the Stars and Stripes into Richmond. Old men and women who had lived their lives in slavery tottered up to the African-American soldiers and exclaimed, "Thank God that I have lived to see this day!" In at least one case this greeting produced an immediate family reunion. The chaplain of the 28th Regiment United States Colored Troops came across an aged woman who inquired if a Garland White was in his regiment as he had been taken from her and sold when he was a small boy. A few minutes of conversation proved that the chaplain himself was her son and he later explained, "I cannot express the joy I felt at this happy meeting of my mother."

As the Confederate capital of Richmond was occupied and, six days later Lee's army surrendered at Appomattox Court House, the bloodiest war in American history came to its fateful end. Almost 200,000 African Americans had put on the blue coat and carried a rifle for the Union cause and over 60,000 of these men never came home. They had paid the supreme sacrifice to make a nation whole again and to end the curse of slavery in a country that had been founded on the principles of liberty.

Glossary

battery	A grouping of artillery pieces; an artillery unit within an army.
bluecoats	Term used for soldiers in the Northern Union army during the Civil War because of the color of their uniforms.
Confederate	Citizen of the Confederate States of America; a Southerner during the Civil War.
Confederacy	The Southern states that seceded from the Union formed a new country called the Confederate States of America also called the Confederacy.
Emancipation Proclamation	A proclamation signed by President Abraham Lincoln on January 1, 1863, declaring the freedom of all persons held in slavery in the rebelling Southern states.
Federals	A name used for members of the Union.
graycoats	Term used for soldiers in the Southern Confederate army during the Civil War because of the color of their uniforms.
ironclads	An armored naval vessel.
Negro	Term used for African Americans in 19th century America.
Rebels	Term used for Southerners in the Civil War.
secessionist	Southerners who voted to secede from the Union and form their own republic.
siege	A military strategy usually against a city in which it is surrounded by enemy troops and ships and all supply routes are cut off. Usually used to try to get a city to surrender.
Stars and Stripes	The flag of the United States.
Union	The United States of America.
Yankees	Term used for Northerners during the Civil War.

Further Reading

Cornish, Dudley. *The Sable Arm: Black Troops in the Union Army.* University of Kansas Press, 1987.

Duncan, Russell. *Blue-Eyed Child of Fortune—The Civil War Letters of Col. Robert Gould Shaw.* Avon Books, 1992.

Emilio, Luis. *A Brave Black Regiment.* Da Capo Press, 1995.

McPherson, James. *The Negro's Civil War.* Random House, 1965.

Trudeau, Noah. *Like Men of War: Black Troops in the Civil War.* Little, Brown Co., 1918.

Websites About African Americans in the Civil War

African American Odyssey—The Civil War: lcweb2.loc.gov/ammem/aaohtml/exhibit/aopart4.html

54th Massachusetts: www.nara.gov/exhall/originals/54thmass.html

National Park Service—African-Americans Civil War Sites: www.itd.nps.gov/cwss/aa-sites.html

United States Colored Troops in the Civil War: www.coax.net/people/lwf/data.htm

U. S. Civil War Center—African Americans, Slavery, and Abolition: www.cws.lsu.edu/cwc/links/slave.htm

Index

PHOTO CREDITS
Chicago Historical Society: p. 35; *Harper's Weekly* : pp. 10, 12, 14, 15, 17, 20, 23, 25, 27, 28, 31, 36, 39, 44, 47, 49, 53, 58; Library of Congress: pp. 21, 45, 54, 57; The Lincoln Museum: p. 32; National Archives: pp. 18, 34